POSITIVE INTENTIONS:

A WORKBOOK FOR LIVING YOUR PURPOSE AND PASSION

KAREN VAN ACKER MA

BALBOA.
PRESS

A DIVISION OF HAY HOUSE

Balboa Press books may be ordered through booksellers or by contacting:

Balboa Press
A Division of Hay House
1663 Liberty Drive
Bloomington, IN 47403
www.balboapress.com
1 (877) 407-4847

Because of the dynamic nature of the Internet, any web addresses or links contained in this book may have changed since publication and may no longer be valid. The views expressed in this work are solely those of the author and do not necessarily reflect the views of the publisher, and the publisher hereby disclaims any responsibility for them.

The author of this book does not dispense medical advice or prescribe the use of any technique as a form of treatment for physical, emotional, or medical problems without the advice of a physician, either directly or indirectly. The intent of the author is only to offer information of a general nature to help you in your quest for emotional and spiritual well-being. In the event you use any of the information in this book for yourself, which is your constitutional right, the author and the publisher assume no responsibility for your actions.

Any people depicted in stock imagery provided by Thinkstock are models, and such images are being used for illustrative purposes only.
Certain stock imagery © Thinkstock.

Print information available on the last page.

ISBN: 978-1-5043-6006-7 (sc)
ISBN: 978-1-5043-6007-4 (e)

Balboa Press rev. date: 08/10/2016

Contents

Preface

Desire also makes you willing to become accountable
for your plan, and that makes you more willing
to create the plan you need to win.
—Zig Ziglar

I wrote this book because I have lived.

Through my life, I haven't made the wisest choices but they were my choices and I am happy to say I owned them. While a wild journey, I have grown into someone whom I can admire and love. The one thing my life has taught me is to always focus on the positive. To focus on what is working instead of what isn't working. Giving negative thoughts attention generally leads to those negative thoughts gaining momentum and taking over your life. If you say, "I am having a terrible day. I am having a terrible day. I am having a terrible day.", what kind of day do you think you will keep having? A terrible day! In reverse, if you say "Today is going to be an awesome day! Today is going to be an awesome day! Today is …" You get the point? Chances are you will have an awesome day.

Yes, there will be circumstances and events, completely out of your control, that will their damndest to make your day terrible. But if someone asks you, "How can you say you are having an awesome day when your car was just in an accident?" All you need to answer is "I am having an awesome day even though my car was in an accident." The day must not be ruined by one event or even a few events. It is how you decide to feel about the whole of the day that makes the difference.

Each day I must make a conscious decision to focus only on the positive, find the positive in everything I do, because if I don't, the world will take over and believe me the world can do a great job of helping one focus on the negative. There are many naysayers in the world. Those that will give you reason to doubt and think negative about anything and everything. Social media can be wonderful, but it can also spew out less than positive vibes. Be mindful of who and what you listen to. And if you cannot close your ears to the negative speech, use your inner self's positive karma to turn the negative into a positive.

If I look back at where all this started, this journey of self-awareness and self-growth, I am amazed at how far I have come. I was a single mother with three young children, the youngest born with autism. Life was hard. I had no real education to fall back on, had no way to earn a living, so I thought, and I felt that I had no real quality of life. Friends were few and I didn't feel I had a role model to look up to, to guide and mentor me. I knew I was going through a breakdown but I knew I had to do something to bring myself out of that black hole.

So, I decided to go to school. While a difficult decision, I knew it would be the best decision I would make. And it was. School was tough, I kid you not, but I learnt that I was smarter than I thought myself to be. School taught me many meaningful lessons, life lessons that I will hold close to my heart forever. I was able to retain and learn so much. A new world had opened up to me that I never thought existed. I was in love with school. Even cartoons from my childhood started to have a different meaning through what I learnt from the schooling. I saw everything in a different light. Everything had new meaning for me.

From small beginning, I found that I had a passion for helping others. Now, nearly 20 years later, I am a licensed professional counselor, helping those who are in a similar position to what I was back then. I found my way out of darkness and now I assist many on a similar path to finding their purpose and passion.

Through each stage of my journey, I faced many challenges, however I pushed through these walls and found contentment like no other on the other side. Sometimes I found myself in spaces, which caused discomfort, where I had no idea what to do. I still experience these moments, which is perfectly normal, but the way I work through them is to dig real deep into my spiritual being. I hold onto the uneasiness of that situation or moment and wait for the clarity. This clarity comes to me eventually if I allow the spirit and essence of the problem to lay inside me for a while. It feels like I am stepping into a new space, within my center once I accept the issue and embrace it, a space that allows me to experience life better than I could imagine. This waiting requires much patience but in the end, I understand myself, as well as the situation, better than before.

I use this technique often with myself, have done so over the years and do so now still, as well as with my clients. I will elaborate on these techniques in the book and the tools that I use. To this day, whenever I feel myself slipping into a negative state, again perfectly normal, I use these tools to get me back to my center, to the real 'Me'. I will show you how to use these methods as we progress through the book. Most times, we just need a change. We often grow as we change and we often outgrow old patterns and things. Through my guidance, I hope to identify what you need to change and what needs to stay the same for you. In the end, we will unlock your passion and free your spirit. Now doesn't that sound exciting? Of course it does! This is why you are here.

Ask yourself this question:

Do you wish to know what your purpose is? A purpose that will lead you to your passion, which will help you attract all the goodness that life has to offer?

If your answer was a resounding yes, then read on.

When you follow certain steps to discovering what your passion is, who you are deep down inside and commit to being only that person, through your actions and through what you say, you will indeed unlock the secret to your true happiness. So much will change in your life, for the good, if you just believe in the real you.

Society forces us, most times, to always do what we "should" do, instead of what we were born to do. We look to events, people and places outside of ourselves to find the answers, when the real truth is inside us. Trusting your own instincts is vital to discovering your true you. Living a life that isn't built for you can lead to many negatives and illnesses (physical, mental and emotional). Feeling stressed and uncomfortable are sure signs you are not on the right path. We try to push these feelings aside, telling ourselves that we "have" to do this and we "have" to do that. The little voice of reason and honesty is pushed to one side as our survival instincts set in. We carry on living the life we always have, not realizing that we are essentially killing our real spirit. With every day that goes by while living the life which is the choice of others and society for us, we kill a little bit of our authentic self. But not to worry, one cannot truly kill our real being completely, not at all! We merely numb it and put it to sleep. Here is where you can wake it up by giving it the pure you; a kiss of life.

Through this workbook, together, we will work through understanding the legitimate you. Once you understand yourself fully and completely, your real energy will guide you down the right and true path, the path you were always meant to take. This golden path will lead you to your life's purpose and once you live your purpose, share it with the world, embrace it as your own, you will acknowledge the passion you feel about your purpose. By being passionate about it or about anything in life, you will realize that this is the right way to grow internally and emotionally to enjoy an authentic life.

Living an authentic life means living the life you are meant to live, being true to yourself, giving your spirit what it needs in order to live a life full of vitality and abundance.

When you are passionate, you will see the passion deep in your mind, like a full color picture. You will live it, you will breath it and you will taste it. Passion incites all of our senses, helps us experience life with all of our being. You will see everything with new eyes, clearer and brighter. You will smell the richness of a new life; taste the sweetness of a credible existence; feel the softness of the luxurious fabric that is your new bed and hear the melodic tunes of the life you are meant to live.

Think about Your Desire

Think about desire: desire for another person, a food, a journey or even sleep. When we desire something, we think about it all the time. We cannot think of anything else other than that one thing we desire. We are consumed by it, in every way possible. Desire is pertinent to life. Without desire we will not finish whatever it is we started, we will not pursue that man who gave us a smile, we will not eat that veggie that is put in front of us, nor take that trip that someone suggested. If you do not desire it, you will not do it, or at least you will not do it with passion. And what is the point of doing anything, if you do not do it with passion?

There is saying that I saw in a workplace once, a few years back. It was printed across the wall as you walked into the organization, for all to see. "Are you having fun? If you are not having fun then what are you doing here?" A loose interpretation of desire, but desire has many derivatives, fun being one of them.

If we think about that something or someone that we desire, we generally, will talk about it. When we talk about it, we develop fresh ideas about it. Fresh ideas full of passion and life, fresh ideas that will develop that desire into something out of this world.

Sometimes the things we desire can be bad for us, but this is where you need to go with your gut and feel your way through whether the desirable item or person is good for your universe.

Chapter 1

Who Am I?

"It's a helluva start, being able to
recognize what makes you happy."
—Lucille Ball

Be who you are and say what you feel because those who
mind don't matter and those who matter don't mind.
—Dr. Seuss

Your journey, to discovering your passion and purpose, begins with you taking a long, hard look at yourself. Never easy, but it is necessary as one of your steps to that ultimate authentic life.

The first tool that we will use is **The Johari Window**. This tool was designed by American psychologists, Joseph Luft and Harrington Ingham. The technique is built around you understanding yourself in relation to the world around you. The "window" assists you in finding out how open you are to new experiences and how you can make changes that will eventually lead you to allowing yourself to be open to change and new options. It allows yourself to personally grow and reach that passion and purpose that you desire.

The Johari Window is comprised of four quadrants. These four quadrants are movable, perpendicular lines, which change as you develop an understanding of yourself, your willingness to share that new self with others and as you develop and grow. When you redo the Johari Window a few months later, you will find the entire structure would have changed. Sometimes it is a good idea to repeat this exercise over and over, during different stages of your life and journey. The results will surprise and excite you.

Have a look of the four quadrants here:

Aspects that you and others know about you	Aspects that only others know about you
Aspects that only you know about yourself	Aspects that no one, including yourself, know about you

Block 1 – Aspects That You and Others Know About You

This is where you will list the aspects of your life that you know very well about yourself and that others know as well. These could range from your favorite color, your particular style of clothing, your level of friendliness, your favorite food, your preferred genre of movie or book and also the way others see you. The list is endless, so you may find that you won't fit it all into that tiny block. I suggest that you use a separate piece of paper to list all of these aspects, as best as you can.

What do you know about yourself that others also know about you?

_____

_____

_____

_____

Block 2 – Aspects That Only Others Know about You

This list would consist of aspects that others know about you, but which you may not be aware of. For this you will need to ask a trusted friend, group of friends and/or a few family members who can identify these areas. This may be a tough list to accept. Some people may be nice and tell you that you smile a lot. Others may not be so nice, telling you that you have a sharp temper. While you may be surprised by what you hear, try to not take offense, try to not hold it against the honest party. The truth is what you need and the truth, in those famous words, will set you free. The truth is there to help you learn about yourself and in the end grow. So, welcome these truths with open arms and embrace them for what they are, the real you.

What do others know about you that you don't know about yourself?

_____

_____

_____

_____

Block 3 – Aspects That Only You Know About Yourself

This part of the exercise is where you will list all the aspects of yourself that only you know and are generally unwilling to share with others. As this is purely for your own use, you can keep this private. These could be deep, dark secrets that you have been nurturing for years, like that clandestine affair you had a few years back or when you stole something from the local grocer. They could be superficial something's, like that you pick your nose in private or don't wash your hands after using the toilet. Whatever they are, they will help you understand how you protect yourself and more importantly how protective you are of yourself.

What aspects about yourself do you hide from others?

_____

_____

_____

_____

Block 4 – Aspects That No One, Including Yourself, Know About You

These are secrets that you withhold from yourself as well as from others. These are the secrets I wish you to reveal the most. They are, potentially, a gold mine field, and once we must dig deep to find. This area will produce the greatest gems of self-growth and self-discovery, taking you closer to your higher purpose. It may be hard to think of things that you are told but you don't know about yourself. It requires you to be super critical of yourself and open your mind up to all possibilities. To critically analyze your life is always tough and it means grappling with the aspects you do know about yourself and asking yourself the gut-wrenching question as to whether you do actually believe those aspects are the true you. Perhaps, once you delve deeper inside your psyche you will discover that those beliefs you had, that you thought were important, are, in fact, not. That if you look at the world in a different manner, that you will be that much closer to finding that authentic life you are meant to lead.

What aspects might you still have to discover about yourself?

_____

_____

_____

_____

Now that you have listed all these aspects of yourself, what can we do with them?

Firstly, did anything surprise you that you've discovered while using the Johari Window? If yes, list all of them, right here!

_____

_____

_____

_____

Which of the four quadrants of Johari Window, would you like to explore more deeply?

_____

_____

_____

_____

How does it make you feel when you read the list of aspects your friends and family shared with you?

_____

_____

_____

_____

Is there anything your friends told you about yourself that you would like to change?

_____

_____

_____

_____

What about findings of your friends and family about you? Were you happy for what they have been observing about you?

_____

_____

_____

_____

How do you think, having all this information from the Johari Window can help you?

_____

_____

_____

_____

Chapter 2

ME Myself & I

Discover Who You Are

I must learn to love the fool in me—the one who feels too much, talks to much, takes too many chances, wins sometimes and loses often, lacks self-control, loves and hates, hurts and gets hurt, promises and breaks promises, laughs and cries.
—Theodore Isaac Rubin

We must be our own before we can be another's.
—Ralph Waldo Emerson

There are two huge challenges in life in relation to this journey. The first is figuring out who you are and the second is deciding what you want. Throughout our lives, we try on different outfits and different hats, the outfits being relationships, jobs, friends, journeys, experiences and more. Many people, out there, feel unsatisfied with their lot and surrender to it, deciding that this is all they will ever have. That this life that they lead is a mundane and meaningless existence and that this is all there is for them. How sad! What an awful way to live! It doesn't have to be that way. There is a better way to live. And it starts with your mindset.

As with any journey you embark on, the events, the people, the places and the experiences will be different for each person. How that person engages during that journey will be different from one to another. Your journey in life is just as unique. The road you will travel will tell a story, a unique story and that will be your story. So why don't you let that life journey be filled with passion? Find out what events, people, places and experiences speak to you. What calls to your heart and soul? What fills you with passion? Don't live someone else's life. Don't follow someone else's road or star. Find and then follow your own unique road and your own unique star.

In this next exercise, I am going to ask you a few simple questions to help you to uncover what's important to you. When answering the questions, imagine you have your own personal Genie and can be granted whatever you want without being limited by your age, finances or even time and space. Open your mind to new possibilities. No matter how ridiculous, no matter how far-fetched, no matter how impractical they may be. This list is yours and yours alone. There is no right or wrong answer here. Just new possibilities! Think of this as your life's bucket list, an endless list of all that you wish to do before you die. Are you ready?

Chapter 4

Defining Your Values

When your values are clear to you,
making decisions becomes easier.
—Roy E. Disney

Now, in retrospect, can you remember a moment in your life where you felt your most negative?

_____

_____

_____

_____

What were you doing when this negativity loaded down your body?

_____

_____

_____

_____

Who was with you in this moment, again, if anyone at all?

_____

_____

_____

_____

What were you wearing at that moment?

_____

_____

_____

_____

How did the negative experience, you are remembering, could make you feel at the time?

_____

_____

_____

_____

Describe the entire experience of this negative memory in detail below, again using as many colorful words as possible.

_____

_____

_____

_____

When you think about these memories, what do you remember seeing around you? Describe your surroundings in detail.

_____

_____

_____

_____

What, do you feel, was missing from the picture?

_____

_____

_____

_____

What do the positive and negative scenarios have in common?

_____

_____

_____

_____

The common themes found in the two sets of questions are important. These common themes are your values. How do these values match up against the ones you noted earlier on your worksheet?

_____

_____

_____

_____

If you could only have one of the values that you've identified, which are the ones you could do without?

_____

_____

_____

_____

Chapter 6

Increase the Positive Voices in Your Life

*Dedicate yourself to the good you deserve and
desire for yourself. Give yourself peace of mind.
You deserve to be happy. You deserve delight.*
—Mark Victor Hansen

*The world as we have created it is a process of our thinking.
It cannot be changed without changing our thinking.*
—Albert Einstein

The late author and motivational speaker Jim Rohn famously said, "You are the average of the five people you spend the most time with." So, an important question would be – "Who do *you* spend most of your time with?"

Are the people, you are close to, are supportive to you? Do they have your best interests at heart? Do they pick you up when you are down and stand by you no matter what? Do they point out all your good qualities when you begin to lose sight of them? Do they honestly tell you when you are acting in a manner not becoming or outside of your true nature?

In our modern-day society, we're fortunate enough to be able to choose the people we surround ourselves with, so why would we ever choose people who don't bring us joy?

On a related note, how do you choose to spend the majority of your time? Do you sit in front of the television for hours? Do you read sensational news stories that make you feel worried, anxious, or stressed?

What you put into your mind is what stays there. Your mind doesn't care what you put there. If it can get rent, it will take it, no matter whether it is a negative or positive thought. As before, what you say to yourself, is what will be reflected in your everyday life. So, it makes sense, that reducing your exposure to negativity from outside sources will raise your feelings of security. And your self-esteem is directly affected by how safe you feel in the world. If your self-esteem is suffering, you won't have the confidence or energy to step outside your comfort zone and create an authentic life. And stepping outside of your comfort zone is what you have to do in order to achieve the perfect lifestyle.

I strongly suggest, as I do, to read books by authors who write about positive psychology and self-motivation. Authors such as Louise Hay, Wayne Dyer, Norman Vincent Peale, and Marianne Williamson, to name just a few. These authors' writings demonstrate that you have power over how you think and feel and—accordingly—how you live your life. Incorporate the voices of these and other positive-minded authors into your life by taking fifteen to twenty minutes every day to read their works. You can also watch inspirational and empowering videos on YouTube and other websites if you have access to the Internet. Using tools such as these to reduce the negativity in your life and increase the positivity, will give you the energy and vision you will need to change your way of being.

It is important to know that some people will voice their opinions as you start to make changes. They are normally the people who are unsatisfied with their own lives. They will see the changes you make as a reflection of their own inability to make changes to their lives. Listen to the positive people only and ignore the negative ones. This is your one life, and you must make the most of it. No matter how challenging it will be, no matter what others may say, stick to what your heart and deep inner soul is telling you.

Answer these questions that follow with all your honesty -

Who in your life is a positive voice? Who is that person or persons in your life, who bring about a feel-good reaction every time you are around them?

_____

_____

_____

_____

Who in your life is less than supportive? Who is that person or persons who make you feel down and sad, who drains your energy every time you are with them?

_____

_____

_____

_____

To work through this chapter, I will need you to answer these next few questions, again as honestly as you can. The answers to these questions will help you work out who the right people are in your life and those who are not doing any good for you.

Do the people you spend the most time with seem happy and successful?

_____

_____

_____

_____

Are they still doing what they have always been doing, and, if so, do they seem to be stuck?

_____

_____

_____

_____

What do these people offer to your life?

_____

_____

_____

_____

Do they lift you up? Do they support you doing things that are good for you? And do they tell you when you are doing things that are not good for you?

_____

_____

_____

_____

Do they, themselves, seem to be working toward their own self-improvement?

_____

_____

_____

_____

Are they successful in their own right and are they helping you, where they can, to also be successful?

_____

_____

_____

_____

If you could create a dream-team group of friends, who would they be and why?

_____

_____

_____

_____

How would they look?

_____

_____

_____

How do you think they would give back to society?

_____

_____

_____

_____

What do they do for fun? What activities do they take part in that they desire and bring them great joy?

_____

_____

_____

_____

Where do they live, work, and create?

_____

_____

_____

_____

How do they support you?

_____

_____

_____

_____

Chapter 8

Developing Your Own Voice

Everyone has that inner voice, the one that's a Negative Nancy. I'd say to ignore that voice and to be confident and follow your heart.
—Katharine McPhee

Your inner voice is the voice of divinity. To hear it, we need to be in solitude, even in crowded places.
—A. R. Rahman

the confidence that comes from that achievement will help make your life more authentic, more peaceful. You will be able to relax knowing that you have arrived.

4. Use Positive Visual Imagery to Create Positive Outcomes

In your mind, picture yourself, as you want yourself to be. Maybe it's successful in business; maybe it's beautiful or happily married. Whatever is the perfect image of yourself is how you should be imagining it. Don't let anyone or anything around you dictate, what is wrong and right way to best imagine your perfect self.

This imagining may take some time, but keep at it. It is a work in progress. You are a work in progress. Define how you see your real you. Practice this visualization every day for a few minutes and you will find changes happening. We often think we don't have time to get quiet and visualize our goals. We live in guilt that giving ourselves those few moments alone, those few minutes to reflect and keep still are selfish. But in fact, it is selfless. We can take these few moments anywhere and anytime. Perhaps while traveling to work, while feeding the baby, in the shower or while waiting for the clothes to dry, even while washing the dishes.

My point is to find a few minutes to visualize yourself where you want to be. Create that picture of how you see yourself physically as well as spiritually, living that perfect life. It is amazing to finally see yourself for who you really are. You are amazing. You are as you see yourself.

5. Set High Expectations for Yourself

If you shoot high, you will hit high. Have you ever heard of that self-fulfilling prophecy? That is the **Galatea** effect. It means that what you believe comes true. Are you believing in good things, because what you believe will, eventually come true?

As cliché as it may sound, when setting goals, reach for the stars. If you miss, you will still be in the same place. If you never try, you will still be in the same place. So why not try and try hard. You deserve to have everything you want. You just have to believe you deserve it. And, trust me—you do!

6. Think Like an Optimist

Optimism is the practice of finding the positivity in any situation. If you're discussing something or explaining it to someone, use positive language and a positive tone. By talking positive you will, in turn, bring positivity into your life. In counseling, we use a tool called reframing to change our thoughts to more positive ones. If you take a negative thought and turn it around to something more positive, you can change your complete emotional state. It is really that simple! Or is that tough?

Rational Emotive Behavioral Therapy teaches us to change our thoughts from fear-based thinking to strength-based thinking. For instance, "I am so afraid I will lose my job" fear based thoughts like this can be debilitating. Change that thinking to "Wow, if I leave this job I will have time to do something I really want to do." This way of expressing the same thought is less emotional, which causes us to exhibit less stress-related behavior. If you use this method whenever you talk to or about yourself, you'll find that your perspective will change over time.

Try the following experiment: Commit to not saying or thinking anything negative about yourself for twenty-four hours. See if this changes how you look at life and what happens in your life going forward.

7. Strive For Peak Performance

Experiencing peak performance over time leads to self-actualization. To rise to your optimal performance level in any area of life, you must be completely focused on what you are doing. What you do every day transforms who you are. If you are sloppy, lazy or doing only half as well as you could, you are not going to reach peak potential.

Having said that, you cannot be perfect overnight. It takes commitment and practice but you might be surprised to know that it only takes 21 days to establish a new behavior and 21 days to break a bad habit. Think of all that would become second nature to you next month if you just started today.

Another aspect to consider in achieving your peak performance is your health and wellness. If you're eating poorly and not getting enough exercise, you won't be able to function to the best of your abilities. This does not only apply to your physical achievements, like sport, but also your everyday life. Just simple walking, sitting, talking, concentrating and performing your work and family duties, will all become easier with a balanced and healthy lifestyle.

What you put into your body is the only fuel it has for generating new cells. If you eat food that isn't nutritious or wholesome, your body and mind won't be able to operate the way you need it to. Self-care is an important part of a prosperous lifestyle. Eat correctly, exercise often, get enough rest, spend time with positive friends and family members, and balance your life as best you can.

Peak performers know that without self-care you can't become your best self. You can't get water from an empty bucket. Garbage in, garbage out. Fill up with goodness so that it can overflow for others. You are the best project you will ever work on!

8. Cultivate Resilience

Everyone has the right to be human. We are human, after all. But what does being human mean? If you make a mistake, well, so what? That's how many of us learn, by our mistakes. It's perfectly okay to make a mistake as long as you get back up and try again. So long as we learn from mistakes we will grow. No one knows how to do anything correct the very first time. But know this. If you find yourself keeping company with people who won't forgive you your mistakes, who expect you to always do things perfectly the first time, who judges you, you may want to consider changing your social group. If changing your social group isn't possible, make sure you find ways to support yourself in a positive way and ignore the naysayers.

Accepting reality, striving to improve yourself, leaning on your support network, and finding creative solutions to problems help you become resilient, which is a key component of being self-confident.

Chapter 9

Control You're Anxiety with Guided Imagery

*Everyone thinks of changing the world, but
no one thinks of changing himself.*
—Leo Tolstoy

*The snake which cannot cast its skin has to die.
As well the minds which are prevented from
changing their opinions; they cease to be mind.*
—Friedrich Nietzsche

For the next exercise, I want you to get real comfortable. (You might want to play some of your favorite soothing music and find a relaxing spot to sit or lay.) As you settle into your relaxed state, know that you are safe and loved, and allow yourself to feel excited and positive.

Feel yourself slipping into a space where you're free to be yourself; where there is no worry; where there is no sorrow; no one is judging you; and there is nothing to fear. Here you can explore the feeling of peace that comes from being fully in the moment. You have the universe at your fingertips and can have everything that's meant to be yours. Believe in the power of your spiritual self to hold you close and safe, and believe that you are loved. From this secure vantage point, you can open your mind to the possibilities of positive change. This is still your place, your safe place. The place where you can open yourself up to all that the world has to offer you. Feel the stillness. Feel the peacefulness. Feel the inner you, the real you, the authentic you.

Like with that Genie from earlier, consider for a moment what life would be like if you had a magic wand. The lack of money wouldn't be an issue. You wouldn't have any doubts. You could throw away the "Yes, buts" and the "What ifs". You could accept what is rightfully yours. Only positive thoughts would enter your brain, and from those thoughts, you would create the life you want for yourself.

Look deep inside yourself, and then write down what you see there by answering the following five questions:

If you could wave that magic wand, what would you be doing professionally?

_____

_____

_____

_____

Where would you be living?

_____

_____

_____

_____

Whom would you be living with?

_____

_____

_____

_____

What would you do with your time outside of work?

_____

_____

_____

_____

What would you contribute to the world?

_____

_____

_____

_____

Most of us have the habit of collecting stuff. The "stuff" is simply a filler for the things we are missing in our life, and we need to clear out this stuff—the thoughts, the emotions, the people— that no longer improve our circumstances. We need to make room for the things we truly want and need.

Organizing experts often say that, when cleaning out your home or closet, if you haven't used something in a year, get rid of it. Go through your things and either donate or throw out all the items you never use and are no longer necessary.

You can do the same with the "stuff" in your life too.

Take a look at your friendships. Do the people you spend the most time with lift you up and support you? If not, can you decrease the amount of time you spend with them and incorporate time with the more positive, inspiring people you identified earlier?

How about your thoughts? Are they helpful or hurtful with regard to your personal growth? Can you let go of the way you currently look at the world and allow for change in your personal worldview?

Try this little exercise. Take one aspect of your life and decide to restructure it so that it better suits the way you want to live. For example, if your finances are making you unhappy, figure out a way to cut your spending or increase your income. If you are debt-free but your finances are disorganized, get a better handle on how much money you have currently, how much money you earn and where it all is allocated.

Living a successful and prosperous life doesn't necessarily involve having lots of stuff. In fact, most of the people who live an abundant life *don't* have a lot of stuff—they simply have the things they truly need or want, and the things that bring them true joy. When you have a lot of stuff you have to insure it, maintain it, and worry about it. Less stuff means less mental and physical pressure.

You also don't need a lot of money to live a prosperous life. You just have to understand what you need in order to *feel* prosperous, and then you have to work to make that your reality. Following your purpose and passion will almost certainly create feelings of prosperity in your life.

As you begin to incorporate all that you've learned about yourself and what it is you truly want and need in life, you'll begin—both consciously and subconsciously—to change your behavior which will in turn help you accomplish your goals. Taking the time to learn about your true self is an accomplishment. Congratulate yourself on a job well done, and accept the gift you've given yourself.

> *"Better indeed is knowledge than mechanical practice. Better than knowledge is meditation. But better still is surrender of attachment to results, because there follows immediate peace."*
> **—From the Bhagavad Gita**

Chapter 11

Focusing on What is Right with "Me"

I am beautiful

"Beauty is not in the face; beauty is a light in the heart."
—Kahlil Gibran

"Knowing yourself is the beginning of all wisdom."
—Aristotle

Are you aware that every person is born with their own gifts, their very own talents and skills? It is true. Each one of us has something that we do well and give as a gift to humankind. Even those that seem to have no purpose other than to antagonize us bring something to this life, to this world.

We may look upon certain people and wonder what their purpose is, what good can they bring to this life, to your life. Perhaps it is through these people that we learn certain lessons, lessons we would not have learned if not for them. A difficult pill to swallow sometimes, especially when we dislike that person, but if you take a proper look at the situation, at the person and what has transpired around them, how they have affected you, you may see the reason they are in your life.

On my own journey and when working with clients on theirs, I have taken the time to write down 50 things that I like about myself, and I encourage my clients to do the same. When making this suggestion for their homework, I usually get a very odd look from them. They all seem to struggle with the idea that there could even be 50 things they would like about themselves. After all, they come to me, to like themselves better. Never the less, I assign the task.

When we are pushed to look for those things positive in ourselves, a shift begins to occur. When we were younger, as a child, we started to realize that the world was telling us who it wanted us to be, what is acceptable and proper. Most of the time, those expectations were in direct opposition to who we were, who our true selves were. If we accept the world's options for our life, we will eventually forget those important aspects about ourselves that we were born with.

So, now I ask you to take on that daunting and confusing task of writing down 50 things that you like about yourself. Don't limit your list. It could be anything, from those that you like a little to those that you love a lot. Maybe you have perfect toes, or love your eyes, or you make the best meatloaf on the planet. Maybe you are able to know exactly what ails an engine just by placing your hand on it, while it hums and vibrates under your touch.

Take your time with this assignment. Don't rush! Dig deep. Dig deep down to the barest part of your soul and be as honest as you can with yourself. This list is for you and you alone. No one needs ever to see it. You may surprise yourself, once you get stuck into this task, that you just may list more than 50 things.

Chapter 12

The Outcome of Your Outcomes

Finding your passion is not just about careers and money. It is about finding your authentic self. The one you have buried beneath other people's needs.
—Kristin Hannah

By now, you should be excited to start applying all that you have learned in the last 11 chapters. That is good. Hold onto that energy, that enthusiasm! Passion is what we want! Passion will propel you to your purpose!

This is a wealth of information and to be sure you are not feeling a little shell shocked, lets break it all down for you.

You've learned in depth, all the angles of who you are, how you see yourself, how the rest of the world sees you; and you have discovered some surprising gems about yourself. Discovering who you are and what you love was the key here. You would have made a long list of all that excites you, all that makes your heart beat that little bit faster and you have worked out how to incorporate these into your life today. Now you know what your core values are. These values help you understand what drives you, what focuses you to be the best person you can be.

Identifying your passion started from when you were a child and we asked you to remember moments when you were feeling extremely positive and also very negative. The common themes gleaned from both would relate to your values and where you should be channeling your energies. Who you spend most of your time with will greatly affect your outlook on life and especially your own life. Building positive forces around you and surrounding yourself with people who inspire, motivate and support you is crucial.

Not only should positive people surround you, but also those people should be advantageous to your goal, your goal, being to find your purpose and live it passionately. You have learned to deal with vast range of matters, from educating yourself in that one special area you are good at to listening to your positive voice. When you do what you are passionate about you want to be able to talk about it with confidence. Setting high goals and tapping into more positivity by using visual imagery is the key to this step as well. And lastly, you learned that it is fine to make mistakes so long as you learn from those mistakes and keep going strong, focused on your most important goal.

Taking your mind and body into a space where only 'you' reside is powerful. Allowing yourself to block out everything but what you feel inside will help you focus on what is most important to you. It is all fair and well to want a change but if you do not create the space for the change to happen, it will not happen. A little cleaning and clearing out is what is necessary. While this can be tough, it is paramount in your journey to an authentic life.

In summary, finding your true passion and purpose is a work in progress. It will not happen overnight. You will not wake up tomorrow, after reading this book, thinking you have discovered the secret to your true happiness. You will not open your eyes and have an epiphany of what your future will look like. You will not step out of your door and be a whole new person. If only it could be that simple. But no, this journey is exactly that, a journey, an expedition, a voyage. See it as an adventure. Your own personal adventure, where you will learn amazing facts about yourself, about other people, about the world you live in and about all that makes up this universe.

This sounds deep and daunting, but it need not be. From these steps you discovered here, you will learn to open up your heart, your soul and your body to new experiences, new ideas and to new people. Some of these will be scary and even exciting at the same time. It is up to you to apply what you have learned here to know which of these experiences, ideas and people are the genuine things thatwill be good for you and which will create a negative vibe inside of you.

You will make mistakes, that is a given, but this does not mean you have failed. Allow yourself these errors, these little indiscretions, because these will assist you on your journey to that ultimate authentic life that is meant just for you.

In a final ending, take a deep breath and congratulate yourself on completing these tasks and know that you can always come back to this workbook, because that is what it is, a workbook of your life. Make notes; rewrite notes and re-read chapters, as you are a work in progress. And that is okay.

I hope that you have learned much from me and will always hold all this close to your heart. Continue to believe in yourself and know that there are many people out there in much the same position as you. You are not alone but you are special and unique.

Never forget that!

Printed in the United States
By Bookmasters